EL

Otro

Lado

Poems by Cecilia Medellin

ISBN: 9798991125000

Published by Alegria Publishing

Illustrations by Elizabeth Medellin

For my beautiful daughters Alejandra and Monica, who make me proud and inspire me to push the boundaries

Table of Contents

WETLANDS
Spruce Goose Runway
Playa Vista Bluff
90094

CANCER DANCER
Hooked
The Buckets
Cancer Dancer

EL OTRO LADO
I Am/*Yo Soy*

Mexican Kiss

Cecilia Medellin

Corn Flakes Shoes /Walk to America

market cereal aisle resole my soul
green rooster my insoles' paradox
pour the grains to swim the bowl
eat the sweet flakes trim the box

praying children on Sunday's altar
we hid our feet against a wall
holy shoe soles expose the holes
dirt brown dots imprint our socks

at home we cut tomorrow's walk
from the corn flakes carton box
curved to fit each child's foot
right and left for sister Nannette

"*mama,* they feel like brand new shoes!"
"they are so shiny, we are so rich!"
the Sun and Moon pyramids blink
standing taller only her Mexican kiss

we emptied our daily sand gather
and treaded light to ride the burden
our feet pebble dented blistered forth
never pussyfooted a dreamer's road

that southern soil we proudly brought
your beacon light rained on our drought
from South to North Ascension Day
you soon became our sweet pancake

this foreign land brought us new joy
rushing to ease our childhood song
we dressed ourselves in northern cloth
and learned to gallop a bucking horse

Cecilia Medellin

our fingers fit your Yankee glove
we hand crocheted unyielding pride
an English tongue with different folk
an Aztec moon a Rushmore song

Vons cereal aisle stroll at sixty-nine
my heart is shouting "hello old soles!"
hello *amigos* the rooster crows
we go so deep you taste so sweet
my old land's shoes re-kiss my feet

Girl On A Bike /Other-Sided

on two wheels I cross over to this bordered land
no desert or wasteland nor swim at Rio Grande
to the other side I aim my bicycle wheels
no fees no coyotes just dismounting right on you

1968 fourteen biting my churro belting Susie Q
a transistor radio blasts Creedence Clearwater
with no brakes I skid to this land's foreign scenes
I am singing and pedaling my immigrant dreams

to the beat of a chatty graveled dirt road
the Mexican pebbles reshape on my soles
the earth's asteroids dismount my green
a Hail Mary crossing this American Dream

I wanted to change my red white and green
I'm riding exhausted seeking out your blue
I meet you betroth you we toast with agave
I'm here other sided convexing your concave

my rosary praying and kissing your soil
my daughters I'll gift you my poems bestow
I'll never backpedal I'll saddle your coast
I'll slide my cold hand inside your warm glove

New Land

your blue got blue-greened
by my border crossing
my green got green-blued
by knowing you
my ancient cactus
eagle green
in my daughters
has appeared
along with their blue
it sits blue
it sits green
to ponder our dream

Cecilia Medellin

L.A.

on you hooked for good I step in your groove
I lay on your dirt in love with your moves
my eyes embrace your eyelash blink
from your mammary gland I happily drink

Bloody Rose

Cecilia Medellin

Ando Mala

icy morning bloody train
southern border hurricane
a coming of age *Domingo*
companion rushing flamingo

I sit refusing to grow
with a *señorita flow*
nature and I disagree
I would rather climb a tree

Llorona wailing a colic
ayyy ayyy ayyy ayyyyyy
no one here to intervene
just before I turn thirteen

ando mala mala mala
ando mala mala mala
a girl imprinted in red
a day upon ill prepared

childhood games far behind
time to cut a hand-me-down
on the rag I'm on the rag
can't buy pads mama said

I cut it to angle a perfect rectangle
I'm folding the ends recalling my friends' tales
when it happened their "I'm bleeding" joy
unlike them I'm sobbing reluctant to grow

I'm needing to learn my ancestor ways
to use dry corn husks? folded *maguey*?
a feathered girl Aztec meanders her chant
she's bleeding with ease on ancient lands

Aztec *Xochitlicue* on top of me she's landing
the red quetzal mark my body commanding
the soil's getting tinted with future child birth
the flooding engulfing the cut green rectangle

I climbed the peach tree big sister could see
I just joined her journey "what's up" puberty
I prayed to the Virgin that I would be spared
I broke out with songs that my girlfriends sang

I was riding on my bike when it happened
— It just happened
I was eating *chicharrones* when it happened
— It just happened
I was galloping my horse when it happened
— It just happened
I was having a big tantrum when it happened
— It just happened

ando mala mala mala
ando mala mala mala
ando mala mala mala
ando mala mala mala

Epicenter

virginity
diluted lie
swallowed whole
digested not eliminated
petrified inside fossilized
purity lie gulped down carefree
by other *mujeres* in Baja with me
we rolled up our tongues
swallowing our pride
looked down
at our hombres
machismo
squinted
eye
and so
it
began
a search for a place which holds in itself a woman's grace
angular dimension lower chakra skin ridge strata
converging colliding shut
packaging the main fold
pivotal place sentinel
a trophy of fools
virginal layer macho man's hold
a sentinel king a purity thing
abyss
there's no fold in us
our plates did not fuse?
our horse rides unglued?
young girls *amigas*
tell your *cariño santo* on your bridal night
that your jug broke playing hide and seek

that your bloody rose of honor
will not embroider his mattress
tell your *cariño santo* to stop hanging
pride red sheets on the patio's daffodils
that
you are a woman
and your worth
lies in your
capacity
to
love

Red Shoes

hanging from a closet hook
they are itching for my feet
to bring out a rhythmic stomp
squeezing out a dormant ploy
syncopated floor heel-toes
about our patriots and foes

missing the throbbing embrace
skin tight fit on my arched feet
rhythmic rebel incantations
spanking the floor unafraid
where ten toes gladly meet
skin fusion bovine and mine

blistered feet immigrant soles
callous blistered, *ampollados*
my blood feeding its creases
with cravings for a new home
hot *punteados, taconeados*
slapping heel-toe *bravados*

the audience shouts *ayayay*
lusting on the dusty stomp
shaking out their dormant joy
unrestrained the eagle fuels
flaps its wings to fan the heat
while my skirt uncurls a swirl

on the wood plank floor above
ten yards circling take a bow
sweaty kisses from first row
a Tenochtitlan snake has bitten
my goody two red *zapatos*
making scandals venom smitten

two hamstrings propelling engines
the thunderous TACA TACAS
the audience dizziness cadence
the *Ajuas* the *Ayyy Ayyy Ayyys*
they're waking with a staccato
the mummies in Guanajuato

shoe talkers of revolution
give a treat to my foot bone
at age fifteen, in the zone
TACA TACA TACA TACA
TACA TACA TACA TACA
TACA TACA Kisses Blown

Cecilia Medellin

Sleepwalking

El Rosal

a rodeo of strife a ranch named *Rosal*
a horse *"Pajarito"* to gallop our land
a motherless deer *"Tepegua"* to feed
a chocolate chicken to chase six small feet

Estrella the dog to kill four-nose snakes
an engineer cowboy who's reading Tolstoy
a four-posted bed to dream and to pray
a cattle hooved throttle with stumbling flair

the oil lamp glare is spooking our hair
a beer bottle castle will stack my despair
warm eggs from the coop a red water tank
a bubbly milk bucket and swing to propel

the emerald bugs will buzz in the air
a rusty nail hangs the newspaper squares
small-medium-large outhouse a girl just fell
"I sat on the big throne like papa" she said

ranch men are busy branding the bulls
we Jeep to the river to swim with cows
riding *Pajarito* until the night comes
we'll eat *tamarindos* as soon as we're back

Germanic word phrases a Tampico beach
oysters at *la playa* shell sucking we reach
a branded girl dowry in sister thread sewn
sleepwalking the rain it came when it came

a large green tamale on Sundays we ate
tequila was pouring from cactus *maguey*
"Bola" pet chicken cluck pecked our heads
he's singing huapangos swallowing the pain

tucked tightly sweet bread on day of the dead
los viejos are dancing we're under the bed
Huasteca violins make dents on our chins
the strings try to lasso the throbbing within

the lessons we learned propel us to sing
the sadness bestowed the love that we shared
It's eighty degrees mom's singing *Cri Cri*
we're sisterhood hugging in Mexican pink

Los Medellin

carved out of a sharp Kimberlite stone, us siblings
pebble floaters scavenged for Bernardo's diamonds
we amalgamated into each other to find our grit
igneous crystals 1953 1954 1955 1958 1959 and 1964

soft brown-eyed vessels and secret fog keepers
storm petrel birds navigating a Mexican gale
hiding inside the ship's lee to stowaway clear
while Maria Luisa's prayers softly steered

fossilized unto us his bruises funneled our steps
stone doughnut hole siblings sometimes rough-edged
in need of some repair floating upstream we went
yearning for circumference looping somewhere

despite the road's roughness our diamonds shined
hermanos y hermanas of you I am so proud

Postpartum

I carry the night under my breath
I carry the night under my dance
I carry the night under my jokes
I carry the night under my laughter
I carry the night under my nightly days

Our Tapestry

Maria Luisa

I lived inside you so glad
rollercoasting your loops
harmonizing our heartbeats
a floating fetus of you in awe

I lived reborn as your child
exhaling your held up breaths
kneeling and praying our blues
singing *huapangos* in Veracruz

our tapestry was completed
a weave of God's love relentless
and because I was your child
I carried you through my life

you are leaving me now
I'll inhabit you no more
forgetting how to exhale
you're refusing my inhale

mother bless your second child
two dancing *huapango* hearts
your love I'll never dismount

Cecilia Medellin

Bernardo

the night I forgave you father
I began to love myself
six months pregnant

like a child crawled into your bed
I didn't have to get married
 to stay home and birth my girl

I didn't have to leave town
Alejandra would be born
giggles singing giggles rained
her dear Abito you became

Alejandra Maria

Alejandra Maria Earth goddess *Coatlicue*
you were born *embadurnada de amor* with Frida strength
amor de luna we gave you
you gave us hope *dulce Esperanza*

a work of Art built by God
with goodness and ancient soul knowledge
una niña llena de sabiduria
first love of my life *hija primogenita*
a miraculous sculpture you are
un Milagro

Tlaloc irrigated and encrypted your spine design
to be the main pillar
until the day the cradled seed went rogue
like a serpentine it coiled twisting your bone

Alejandra you were rebuilt by man reshuffled and uncoiled
sewn upright with hooks screws and cold stainless steel rods
never to be the girl with the twisted back

they embrace your softness as you lay
atornillada with the vertical obsidian scar in your back
no mortar needed for you are cemented nailed and glued shut
with your own sweet bone shavings dipped in *maguey* juice

it was not the eagle but you Alejandra who ate the cactus fruit to
construct
your amazing and valiant *corazon de tuna*
which bleeds for the marginalized
corazon que sangra por los tuyos
your *cuento* is not told through Aztec *codices*
it is told by your soul

you wear your battle scars with pride
to give hope to others
your hips swivel to the rhythm of a *Tenochtitlan sonajeros*
dance
your Aztec princess voice meets Ariel's love song
to give voice to our youth
you toil you strive
never asking how many steps to climb
your love rivers in my veins
play me a love song piano girl

You are not the princess
You are the
Pyramid

My First Ojitos/9-20

my crimson hand upon your blue
soft lash brown eyes making *"ojitos"*
teal minded child my first daughter

glad to hopscotch your *bebeleche*
you are my sweet *arroz con leche*
my corn flake shoes pointing North

singing *Cri Cri* with your Beauty doll
galloping "ponies" and "patis" road
a stack of giggles and stories told

roll the tortillas with your Abi
tightly tuck the *carne asada*
appapachandote Mexican style

at your piano Twinkle Star
a sweet *buñuelo* you are

Gift

young and old First and Onlys
recognize their struggles penned
your visit brings them new hope
your gift befriending their road

my dearest Harvard Latina
producer of hugs and kisses
Alejandra Maria Amor
a blessing for us all

Monica's Blessing

inside my womb no wiggle room
a heartbeat rides a meringue pie
not born yet, she is treading water
wet lips hot skin seeking a mother

pum pum mom pum pum pum girl
eyes and curls knitting brown hues
shantytown blistered belly cocoon
a rhythm swings to Chinese herbs

pum pum prance pum pum our dance
untangle us undoing the skillful loops
time to meet! Sufficient hues!
over upon me the nine month stride
growing life no longer a wife

a bareback sway a dolphins' pride
informs your glide and water ride
I greet and kiss my second girl
July the seventh at three and dime
and so it went the second time

oh the merengues we'll dance together
oh the tortillas we'll eat with butter
you just arrived covered with dreams
I'm singing softly my ocean girl
finally here! Lassoing your mother

Cecilia Medellin

Girl On A Board

2008 fifteen, a *quinceañera's* mermaid tail
Pacific coast rider slide on your wet gown
your Baja ancestors keep seeking your gnarly
like rooster tails on a lime seagrass morning

you weave your hair with sapphire tresses
you saddle and lasso the waves at your fiesta
bareback ocean cowgirl sweetening the salty
a rolled-up tide billow persuading your punchy

the sea floor shines on you its globigerina
barnacle plating your breast scars
the broken shells knitting a strong cast
Creator of Surf Girls and rip curls

Monica most rare vaquita, Cortez Sea snuggled
immigrant's daughter crushing barriers riding 90
the sea craves your *ceviche* scented skin
and your calamari curls twirling Pacific swirls

euphoric zone maiden in your watery *hacienda*
embracing of women you focus your generous lens
on the shoreline iridescent water nymph
your warrior spirit let it glow aquamarine
ocean rodeo bronco rider bridling the crystalline

Once Upon A Time In Baja/The Helper

meringue obsessed May
gold awaited lemon day
baking mantra extraordinaire

at Tecate's southern border
a slurping and licking helper
suave Maria mentor baker

baking scrumptious lemon pies
Guerrero Negro egg cartons
a father's pay for a project

my bent tongue rotates the bowl
meringue goo sweetly drenched
yellow mustaching mouth corners

a frosted chin and nose tip
sliding through skinny dip
enjoying their membership

my happy face slowly circles
I need no spoon bottom surfer
my grunting swallowing gurgles

selling the pies mother daughter
new shoes for Bernie my brother
for his birthday we will barter

among the pies we danced mambo
to Perez Prado *bailando*
my best job once upon *cuando*

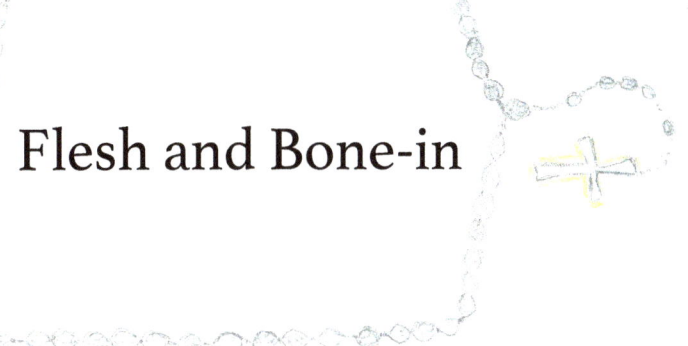

Flesh and Bone-in

Cecilia Medellin

God's Eye

I am letting you spot me as I slide down
I am falling into you, my gaze floating up
not sneaking a peek at the looming abyss
or inquiring about the goodness of your kiss

this time I am not making deadly sure I survive
that your arms are outstretched wide enough
or if you will hold me at the right hip curvature
or if your tent will contain my structure

letting you catch me all flesh and bone-in
as I spiral down my whirly hurricane
until I enter your glorious open Eye
and my fall becomes a gentle shimmer
that composes my best dance piece
the one that lacks all choreography

I become a flying dancing bag
like the one in that American film
the bag embracing your warmth
a twirly dancer all about you, not me
I am finally consenting the impromptu

in the middle of your naked Eye
I quietly recline my chronic pride
navigating your precious lens
abandoned, discombobulated

I'm letting you house me
Your eyebrows, the roof over my head
Your eyelids, with each blink my rocking hammock
Your eyelashes, tropical fans softening the heat
the bags under Your Eyes, where you tuck my hurt

I'm letting you cleanse me
sponging, tear bathing me
ridding me of the chimpanzee
in bed with your sweet tea
weak-kneed, latch-keyed

I'm letting you love me
myself reclined on you
cocooning my marooning
while I lay here crooning

bubbles of love popping
nothing between us fits
your pupil on me gazing
I'm letting you rest me

Azul

53
madres
6 padres
my sadness
regret clutter chain
laying here this L.A. Summer
blue bead my soul 59 me
unplugging my inward fidget
navigating at your sea
chaplet me
dear
G
O
N
D
O
L
I
E
R
reshaping my thumb and pointer
prayer indented skin tips
flutter gazing your eye
to retreat this
numbing
F
R
I
G
H
T
love
dangle
hail marry me
rosary blue my slumber

Cecilia Medellin

usher my fingers heat wave
rattled brained and squeezing hard
your fathers and mothers raining
connecting grace looping lanes
suspending a bleeding brain
a crown of fidgets ablaze
a Mexican churro fiesta
the convex for
your
concave

Cecilia Medellin

Mother

Guadalupe weep on me
Mexican Virgin
brunette
+
+

Last Beach

piggyback rider
no longer a fighter
I jump on your back
hold on to you tight

forgetting the anguish
I whisper in Spanish
tu casa es mi casa
que viva *la raza*

my leg hair scatters
mane loss won't matter
I dare! Who cares!
about all those hairs

my tummy protruding
I toss out the spanks
I'm one of your lambs
submit to your plans

I'm meeting my maker
his sweet tooth's awaiting
I'm caked in his arms
with him integrating ...

when he pings I will pong
when he dings I will dong
when he springs I will sprung
forever his tagalong

my sand dollar's spent
my castle unmanned
my tan gleams complete
amidst the seaweed

the octopus tickles
the urchin's soft prickle
the dolphins are finning
the beach boys are singing

my shells gathered in
to place in your basket
my good and bad deeds
awaiting the casket

I wiggle and giggle
the sand off my eyes
approaching your house
my mouth full of fries

my board has docked
on your island divine
my God, my pride
my piggyback ride

giggle wiggle giggle glide
jiving the ultimate dive

Funny Bone

Limber Tongue

The following documents my licking techniques, beloved lemon mantras, and limber tongue exercises

My "sticking it out" daily routine:

1. The Constellation - no specific tongue method just licking around the bowl with no rhyme or reason (most fun, easy for beginners)

2. The Lollipop Method - up and down slow licks with a break to swallow at the peak while slowly bobbing your head

3. The Cow Lick - (from my Veracruz ranch days) a side to side right and left tongue over the lower lip, twist pendulum-like

4. The Windshield Wiper - (or coming to America in an old Impala in the rain) 180 degree arched tongue over the upper lip sweep (skip if choosing to keep frost mustache)

5. The Taquito Torpedo - (one of my favorites) which showcased my ability to roll my tongue into a taquito shape as I "stick it to the Man" in and out of my mouth

6. The Come Hither or Come On - (my licking masterpiece) which consisted of curling my tongue tip upwards like a hook as if beckoning someone to slowly come forward, a good way to make friends

7. The Slurper - a deep dive to bowl bottom inhaling with both nose and mouth in unison, enjoying the blubbering sound (also good for nose dryness)

At around 15 years of age I became obsessed with boys
I left my pie baking ways behind and grew up (?)

My lemon meringue days will always hold a special place in my mouth. I would love to say that I became a very famous lemon meringue pie baker and that my bowl licking methods were published in many languages, that to this date people teach my techniques

Wasted Nights

Bachata to the bathroom

Bolero to the bowl

Can-Can to the can

Cha-cha my chimichangas

Fandango to Durango

Hustle out the dumplings

Jitterbug the John

Latrine Lambada zone

Merengue hurricane

Montezuma revenge

Plie the souffle

Poets corner scorcher

Porcelain pirouette

Rumba runs

Septic tank samba

Shimmy to the loo

Toilet tart art

Twerking on the throne

The commode my new abode

Unleashing the trombone

Waltzing the chicharron

A tush ambush

A turdy download

Whoosh

Whoosh

Whoooosssshhhh

Zumba to saca saca Zacatecas

Southern California Prayer

now I lay me down to sleep
my swearing bleep I'm yours to keep
septum straight nose me to breathe
please un-cottage cheese my thighs
and scalpel tight this wiggly rump

boob job me to new bouncy perks
butt lift me straight down to Brazil
un-ripple the dimples stretch the swirls
and don't forget to bless the girls

unclench my teeth my tongue release
this jaw clicking sound while I eat cheese
behind my ears do stitch some threads
I'll make amends and turn some heads

duck bill me to a meaty pout
to yearbook days my looks return
on my late face un-droop the loop
please Betty-Boop my greying goop

un-ring my ear's tinnitus shriek
un-blur my eyes from cataracts
spider de-vein my varicose
and rid me of the adipose

un-trigger my finger the one pointing up
re-swivel my hips to a galloping strut
my hemorrhoids shrink with a mighty blink
if in a good mood please throw in the sink

de-bunion my feet to un-kick the bucket
a grand belly stitch will skillfully "tuck it"
my body redo the old one I'm ghosting
we'll toast and post and cook up a roast

I do not mean to cherry-pick
but *por favor!* undo some years!
help my bone loss 'cause you're the boss
we'll pickle ball or play lacrosse

forbid my wrinkles to creep so deep
Los Angeles style while I'm asleep
to heal the trauma I may need weed
or chew some gummies with CBD

if not I'll take a rain check
I'll kiss the ceiling to work my neck
my convex tummy reshape concave
for what the heck some folks still check

Infuse some tears in my dry eye
don't mummify me at 69
I trust you won't you're in the know
salute my eye floaters "El Flutie" and "La Flo"

a crackling knee going upstairs
meniscus tear while at the fair
lalala land May Day nip tuck
Los Angeles style while I'm asleep

sciatica reshuffle my overdramatic rheumatic
not shouting what the heck! is plain diplomatic
I'm missing hormones and feeling quite HOT
to manage it all I'll watch Cheech and Chong.

Amen

Wetlands

Spruce Goose Runway

soaking our struggles blowing spa bubbles
we float up to surface unbuckling our goggles
the kids have long gone to swim their laptops

the purple chairs dwelling the orange's ones yelling
missing are the children their cannonball screaming
but us we are older and playa consorting
too quiet out here we are missing the cheers

we're soaked treading water our fears cavalier
we swim and we lay Resorting the warnings
on this Runway Playa Day

PlayaVista Bluff

the Ballona Wetlands are having a ball
winter crumbles but all I hear is grumbling
few people to host with Coronas ghost
we are not all right we let in the fright

the trees keep birding new trails forking

the lizards give tongue discarding the cold
sparrows bloom the Yerba Santa croons
this looks like spring it should be good
but we didn't make the grade we're scared

the yellow flowers don't know it
the purple flowers don't show it
for them it's color bouncing spring 2020
but Corona keeps lurking and coughing on us
its feverish unmasked desperado rush

Loyola bells are ringing a back-to-school swing
empty desks are missing the students' warm sit
down here we're mourning our comings and goings
Playa Vista Bluff mumbling and rambling across

we're keeping a distance postponing our hugs
despairing with chills we're gasping out here
for someone we meet the trick is six feet
politics can wait we're planning our escape
KN95s, gloved hands but we need to swear

we're getting sweet pickled in our mason jars
gathering our flavor could humble us a while
our lids will twist left and we'll reconnect
the outings postponed will gain new respect

restoring our mounting humanity debt
we could learn to humble our heads
our pride got too big we needed a stumble
to soften our footprint on this jagged Earth

90094

driving south Lincoln
passing The Marina
Playa Vista to our left
my daughters and I dreamt

where Spruce Goose once stood
Seabeach Place my address
we love it out here
at Bluff Creek's feet

Ballona Creek north
our dream brought forth
Westchester bluffs
Wetlands Salt Marsh

all the way from Veracruz
taking off my corn flake shoes
now I'm living where I choose

Cancer Dancer

Hooked

sitting in this Kaiser chair
waiting for my namaste
I am here on chemo day
hooked dripping with CMF
my arm a needle's buffet

singing my life's "In-A-Gadda"
tackling the whole enchilada
on a cactus prick I sit
invasive malignant mass
hangs with me kicking ass

cancer me quieres chupar
y no me dejas gozar
cancer me quieres chupar
chupas chupas chupas chupas
my bones you are sucking dry
cancer me quieres chupar
y no me dejas gozar

the tourniquet tightens
the needle poke's biting
and all I can say is
"que poca madre pinche cabron"
"que poca madre cancer chignon"

the Cytoxan squirt
monotonous drip
my nausea will birth
I'd rather be hiking
Temescal Ram climbing
Skull Rock vista riding

ponme ya el torniquete
ya estoy lista pal piquete

que en mis venas ya se mete
como un pinche reguilete
pues de el yo soy su juguete
me hace bailar el huateque

I'm hoping for strong *aguardiente*
as I feel this *lentamente*

my feathers in disarray
I'm missing my thick curly hair
a balding eagle will rise
tricking death out of breath

crazy bird *pajara loca*
give me an agave day
for I sit on *this maguey*
repeating *"que pasa guey"*

The Buckets

bucket ready evening plight
runs to vomit Sunday night
my nose will begin the dive
I'm preparing for the fight

the *chiles rellenos* evening
will explode with all its might
and the next day *chilaquiles*
will dog fight until midnight
wearing my second pajama
I lay awake in my *cama*

bailarina bailadora
mi Llorona baila baila
La Bikina La Cecilia
baila tus bailes y llora
en la plaza yo me siento
confesando sin aliento
al señor mi sacramento
todo lo que traigo adentro

at Menlo school
there's a whisper
during recess
llora y llora
at Marine street
there's a rumor
that you have cancer
señora

ayy ayy my wails crescendo
no more doubts or innuendo
cancer me quieres chupar
adjusting my repertoire
no me dejas de gritar
cancer *me quieres chupar*

Cancer Dancer

I'm hoping for strong *aguardiente*
as I dance this *lentamente*
I'm hoping for strong tequila
détente cancer détente

valiant ones un-kick your buckets
cancer dancers tell me *cuando*
dancing all night a fandango
strip your clothing go commando

dance us un *Dia De Los Muertos*
with *La Llorona bailando*
I'm dancing with *La Catrina*
at the Zocalo *cantando*
all my blues *zapateando*

show me all your cancer moves
the ones that helped you survive
cancer dancer manifesto
"a pelo" riding bareback

Alejandra la valiente
Monica la valiente
you've become dancers too
embracing your BRCA journey

hasta cuando dancer *cuando*
we'll dance the dance we were given
we will dance it? it will dance us?
must we dance you *hasta cuando?*
hasta cuando cancer cuando
hasta cuando cancer cuando?

El Otro Lado

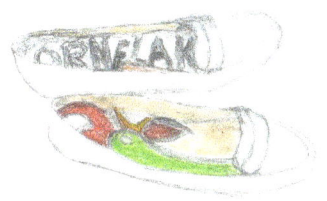

Cecilia Medellin

I Am/*Yo Soy*

I am from *Baja*
I am from *Mexico*
I am from *Juan Gabriel*
I am from *Chicharrones*
I am from *"Mamacita!"*
I am from *Pozole*
I am from *Mexicanos al Grito de Guerra*
I am from *Bolillos*
I am from *El Cuchuma*
I am from *Gansitos Marinela*
I am from *Loteria*
I am from *Pan Dulce*
I am from *Calle Hidalgo*
I am from *Tacos*
I am from *Chocolate La Abuelita*
I am from *Vivora de la Mar*
I am from *Capirotada*
I am from *El Chapulin Colorado*
I am from *Bebeleche*
I am from *El Aguila y Serpiente*
I am *Green White Red missing the Blue*
I am from *Bernardo y Maria Luisa*
I am from *Cecilia Lindo Amorcito*
I am from *seamless diction*
I am from *corn flake shoes*
I am from *Este Lado*

Cecilia Medellin

Yo soy de Alta
Yo soy de America
Yo soy de Creedenc Clearwater
Yo soy de potato chips
Yo soy de "Hey babe!"
Yo soy de Chicken noodle
Yo soy de America the Beautiful
Yo soy de Wonder Bread
Yo soy de Temescal Canyon
Yo soy de Hostess Twinkies
Yo soy del Bingo
Yo soy de doughnuts
Yo soy de Marine Street
Yo soy de Big Macs
Yo soy de Nesquik
Yo soy de London Bridges
Yo soy de Bread Pudding
Yo soy de Cheech and Chong
Yo soy de Hop Scotch
Yo soy de Stars and Stripes
Yo soy de White Red Blue missing the Green
Yo soy de Alejandra and Monica
Yo soy de Cecilia you're breaking my heart
Yo soy de thick accent
Yo soy de tennis shoes
Yo soy del Otro Lado

ACKNOWLEDGEMENTS

To my daughter Alejandra for her inspiration and support in making this book a reality. To my daughter Monica for her supportive feedback and thoughtfulness. To my husband Robert, for his patience and encouragement throughout this process. To my sister Elizabeth for her beautiful illustrations in the book. To my brothers and sisters – Elizabeth, Nannette, Diana, Alfonso, and Bernie - for their love. To my uncle Mario Uribe for showing us the beauty on this "Otro Lado." To my first cousin Mario Rueda for opening his house to us when we first came to Los Angeles. To my editor Estella Ramirez for her helpful feedback and friendship. A special thanks to Davina Ferreira and Diane Castaneda from Alegria Publishing.

ABOUT THE AUTHOR

Cecilia Medellin is a poet, contemporary dancer, and former elementary school teacher in the Los Angeles Unified School District. After immigrating to Los Angeles from Mexico as a teenager, she joined a number of dance companies, ranging from modern dance to Mexican baile folklórico. Cecilia was a principal dancer in a Mexican folkloric dance company founded by former students of Amalia Hernández, the founder of Ballet Folklórico de México. She also choreographed and performed a multi-dancer routine set to her original poem Ando Mala at Santa Monica College. Previously, Cecilia was a kindergarten teacher at Menlo Avenue Elementary School for eighteen years, before retiring in 2017. In her free time, she enjoys writing poetry, hiking, biking on the beach, salsa dancing with her husband Robert, and spending time with her two daughters, Alejandra and Monica.

Cecilia Medellin